TEAM SPIRIT!™

INDOOR PERCUSSION ENSEMBLES AND DRUM CORPS

Daniel Fyffe

The Rosen Publishing Group, Inc., New York

I dedicate this book to my students for the memories; my father, who believed in me; and my family, including my daughter, Rachel, son, Evan, and wife, Sheryl, whose love and support made me who I am today.

Published in 2007 by The Rosen Publishing Group, Inc.
29 East 21st Street, New York, NY 10010

First Edition

Library of Congress Cataloging-in-Publication Data

Fyffe, Daniel.
Indoor percussion ensembles and drum corps/Daniel Fyffe.—1st ed.
    p. cm.—(Team spirit!)
Includes bibliographical references (p.) and index.
ISBN 1-4042-0733-3 (library binding)
1. Percussion instruments. 2. Percussion ensembles—History and criticism.
3. Drum and bugle corps. 4. Drummers (Musicians)—Vocational guidance.
I. Title. II. Series: Team spirit! (New York, N.Y.)
ML1030.F94 2007
785'.68—dc22
2006001729

Manufactured in the United States of America

On the cover: The Troopers drum and bugle corps perform during the Drum Corps International Finals in Orlando, Florida, on August 7, 2003.

CONTENTS

EXHILARATING RHYTHMS

For three months each year, many young people across the United States commit weekend after weekend to performing with indoor percussion ensembles and drum corps. It is a grueling schedule that follows months of intense rehearsals.

Why do they give up this valuable time that their peers use for typical teen pursuits such as hanging out at the mall or playing pick-up games of football, basketball, or soccer? To be sure, the chance to hoist a trophy near the end of the performing (and competitive) season—February through April for indoor percussion ensembles and the summer months for drum corps— is a reason for some. So too are being a part of

Performing for thousands at the Drum Corps International World Championships, the Cavaliers Drum and Bugle Corps wows the crowd with outstanding choreography and musicianship. A five-time winner of the DCI World Championships, the Cavaliers is one of the most prominent drum corps in the United States.

pregame and halftime displays at high school football games and the realistic dream of participating in a large parade, such as the Macy's Thanksgiving Day Parade or the Tournament of Roses.

But the real lure for most is the feeling they get when their hard work pays off in an outstanding performance that wows the crowd. For these players, the time spent is not considered a sacrifice. They have drumming in their blood. The rush of adrenaline, the anticipation before entering the field, the performance, and the release of emotion after a good performance are all the payback they need for the many hours of rehearsals.

As members of indoor percussion ensembles and drum corps, they are part of the exciting world of pageantry. It is a world in which the cheerleaders, dancers, musicians, and other skilled spirit artists—most publicly recognized as the organized supporters of sports teams—take center stage as stars in their own right. Where pom squads, dance teams, majorettes, and band front units provide the razzle-dazzle of the competitive pageantry circuit, indoor percussion ensembles and drum corps (collectively referred to as competitive percussion)—together with marching bands—represent its rhythmic vibrancy.

Like the other pageantry arts, indoor percussion ensembles and drum corps vie for supremacy and bragging rights in local, regional, national, and even world championships. These competitions provide thrilling displays of the musicianship and stagecraft of the nation's finest competitive percussive units. For those who witness

Percussionists represent the rhythmic vibrancy of the pageantry arts. With dedication to their craft, percussionists are able to create complete musical and visual performances that are unique in the world of pageantry.

excited teens entering the field and delivering solid performances to the rapturous applause of appreciative fans, it is no small wonder that so many young people commit their weekends to competitive percussion.

CHAPTER

1

Indoor Percussion Ensembles

An indoor percussion ensemble, or indoor drumline, is a musical performing unit that primarily plays instruments of the percussion family. Sometimes, standard jazz band rhythm instruments, such as a bass guitar, guitar, and keyboard, are added. Typically, a competitive indoor percussion ensemble competes during the months of February through April, though this may vary from region to region.

Indoor percussion ensembles use instruments from all over the world. These instruments are often equipped with carriers and straps to allow musicians to incorporate them into the performance.

A percussion instrument is one that produces sound when it is struck, shaken, or scraped. Percussion instruments are one of the four families of musical instruments. The other three families are strings, woodwinds, and brass instruments. String instruments produce sound waves by the vibration of strings. They include the violin, viola, cello, bass, guitar, and harp. Woodwind instruments, which most often produce sound waves by the vibration of a reed, include the clarinet, saxophone, oboe, bassoon, and flute. (The flute is an exception among woodwind instruments because it does not have a reed.) Brass instruments produce sound waves by the vibration of the player's lips. They include the trumpet, French horn, trombones, baritone, and tuba. String, brass, and woodwind instruments are not used in percussion ensembles.

Types of Percussion

Because most cultures of the world use some form of percussion instrument in their music, the percussion family is a very large and diverse group of instruments. Accordingly, the percussion instruments used in indoor percussion ensembles—and in drum corps—are very diverse and can be great in numbers. Percussion instruments can be divided into various categories: classical, or concert, percussion; marching percussion; combo percussion; and ethnic percussion.

Classical percussion instruments are those that are used by orchestras, concert bands, and indoor concert percussion ensembles. The classical or concert percussion group includes timpani, snare drums, bass drums, cymbals, tambourines, triangles, bells, xylophones, vibraphones, marimbas, and chimes.

Marching percussion instruments are used by high school and college marching bands, indoor movement percussion ensembles, and drum and bugle corps. They include marching snare drums (which are worn by the player using a strap or carrier), multi-tenor drums (three to five drums connected together and worn by the player, sometimes called trios, quads, or quints), marching bass

The marimba is the workhorse of the percussion ensemble. With its wide range of notes and expressive qualities, the marimba is useful in a variety of musical applications. The marimba can be found in a number of cultures, from the continent of Africa to Central America.

drums of different sizes (also worn by the player), and crash (or field) cymbals.

The third group of percussion instruments might be classified as combo percussion instruments, which are typically used in jazz or rock bands. This includes the drum set. Finally, all other percussion instruments can be grouped together as ethnic percussions. These are instruments used by percussionists from Central America, South America, the Caribbean, and Africa. They include conga drums, bongo drums, timbales, steel drums, maracas, claves, cowbells, and a host of others.

Steel Drums

The steel drum (or pan, as it is more correctly known) is a pitched percussion instrument that is made from a 55-gallon oil drum. One of the most recently invented instruments, it originated in the Caribbean island of Trinidad around 1940. Accordingly, it is widely associated with Caribbean music, particularly calypso and soca. However, the steel drum has grown in popularity beyond its Caribbean roots and can be found throughout the United States.

Before steel drums existed, many Trinidadians used bamboo sticks of various lengths to create musical sounds. These were outlawed because street gangs used the sticks as weapons in street fights surrounding Carnival celebrations. The musically talented islanders soon discovered through trial and error that steel drums, when properly treated, can create a musical pitch. Because the United States Navy was stationed at Trinidad, steel drums were readily available.

By sinking the bottom of the pan, pounding out tonal points, and tempering with fire, steel drums were created by master tuners throughout the island. As members of the United States Navy returned to their homes, they brought back information about the steel drums. Soon the popularity of this new instrument spread throughout the Caribbean and the United States.

An annual national steel drum music competition is held in Trinidad. Steel drum ensembles from across the island gather and compete against each other. A wide variety of music including classical, jazz, calypso, and reggae is performed with steel drums.

A steel band orchestra, composed of African American students, perform at a street festival in Brooklyn, New York. Steel drums are common in American urban centers that have large Caribbean immigrant populations.

Competitive Indoor Percussion Ensembles

In the world of indoor percussion competition, there are two main divisions: movement and concert. Indoor movement percussion ensembles (also known as indoor marching percussion ensembles) utilize marching percussion instruments as well as concert or classical percussion instruments. Because marching percussion instruments, such as the snare drum, are worn by the players, the musicians are able to execute complex drill and movement routines. Therefore, indoor movement percussion ensemble performances include both music and elaborate drill movement. Movement ensembles also use costumes and props to add drama to their act. The performance area for the movement ensemble is the size of a basketball court.

The second division, indoor concert (or indoor non-movement) percussion ensemble, uses all percussion instruments except the marching instruments. Also, indoor concert percussion ensembles do not perform drill routines. They move only when it is necessary to change instruments. Consequently, the performance area for indoor concert percussion ensembles may be smaller than that of the movement ensemble. However, for most competitions, the indoor concert percussion ensembles perform and compete in a gymnasium along with the indoor movement percussion ensembles. The attire for the indoor concert percussion ensembles can be matching outfits or formal wear. However, this varies from group to group.

Competitive indoor percussion ensembles strive for perfection. From technique and stick heights to costuming and facial expression, these ensembles prepare every detail of their performance.

Noncompetitive Performances

Indoor percussion ensembles perform in a wide variety of venues outside of competition. Some high school indoor percussion ensembles perform as part of the halftime entertainment during basketball games. Also, some indoor percussion ensembles perform in exhibition at indoor winter guard competitions. Moreover, many state music associations host small ensemble

No matter the performance hall, contest, or concert, playing a percussion instrument is an enjoyable and rewarding experience.

festivals that offer performance opportunities for indoor percussion ensembles, as well as the chance to work with clinicians to improve their skills. In addition, the Percussive Arts Society, an international organization of percussionists, has state chapters throughout the United States and abroad. These local chapters sponsor Day of Percussion events that feature clinicians and performing ensembles.

There are many other noncompetitive performance opportunities for the indoor percussion ensemble. Indeed, the range of opportunities is limited only by the imagination of the ensemble's director. Many indoor percussion ensembles prefer not to compete. Instead, they perform only at noncompetitive events as concert percussion ensembles.

The competitive indoor movement percussion ensemble incorporates many theatrical elements into its show. This type of ensemble presents a performance that uses movement, costumes, props, and music.

Competition History

The history of competitive indoor percussion dates back to the late 1970s, when several regional percussion invitationals (contests) were organized to answer the call of band directors looking for competitions in which to enter their marching band drum lines after the official marching season. Soon cold weather forced contest organizers in the northern states to move some of their competitions indoors. One of the first such

The competitive indoor concert percussion ensemble presents a performance that relies on musical skill without the use of movement and props.

contests was the Moorehead State University indoor drum line competition, which attracted groups from all over the Midwest. Since the mid-1980s, the Percussive Arts Society has held an indoor percussion ensemble competition at its annual international convention. There were also several other competitions being held on the local, regional, and national levels.

Inconsistency in contest rules and requirements quickly became a problem for competing indoor percussion ensembles as they expanded their schedules to attend several independent invitationals. In other words, these contests did not always have the same set of rules. Judges (or adjudicators, as they are called in competitive percussion) from different contests had different philosophies. As a result, the directors of indoor percussion ensembles were often puzzled as to what the judges expected and were evaluating. Indoor percussion ensembles were frequently changing their shows to meet different performance space limitations, timing requirements, and judging philosophies of the various contests in which they participated. The situation remained disorganized until the Winter Guard International (WGI) offered a model that indoor percussion groups could embrace.

Winter Guard International was established in 1977 by color guard directors to organize an international indoor circuit for winter guards. Winter guards are similar to the color guards that are a part of marching bands. Winter guards compete in gymnasiums during winter months, using flags, rifles, and sabers similar to color guards. However, unlike color guards, they perform to taped music rather than to a live marching band. In 1992, Winter Guard International created a division for indoor percussion ensembles, offering indoor percussion competitions at its winter guard shows. Thanks to WGI, indoor percussion competitions became uniform throughout the United States.

Indoor percussion ensembles participating in the Winter Guard International regional and national events quickly realized they needed local competition circuits to perfect their craft before they entered the WGI competitions. By the late 1990s, state circuits were being started throughout the United States.

In order to create a consistent scoring and judging system, many state circuits adopted Winter Guard International rules and procedures. Winter Guard International competitions have divisions set up for both indoor concert percussion ensembles and indoor movement percussion ensembles. Though most indoor percussion ensembles represent high schools, a few junior high school groups are beginning to compete. School-sponsored indoor percussion ensembles compete in Winter Guard International's scholastic divisions.

WGI also has divisions for independent indoor percussion ensembles, which have members from several different schools and sometimes from several different regions of the country. The rules for the independent indoor percussion ensembles are the same as the rules for the scholastic or high school indoor percussion ensembles, except for a rule concerning age requirements and school affiliation. Members of independent percussion ensembles may be between the ages of fourteen and twenty-one.

The Music

The collection and musical arrangements of the compositions that an indoor percussion ensemble plays is known as the musical book. It can be as varied and as colorful as the groups themselves. Indoor percussion ensembles are capable of playing nearly every form of music, including orchestral transcriptions, jazz arrangements, rock tunes, hip-hop, Latin or salsa tunes, steel drum or calypso arrangements, and, of course, tunes written exclusively for percussion ensembles.

Musical compositions used in noncompetitive settings are typically available to the general public and can be purchased from publishers. On the other hand, for most indoor percussion ensembles, the compositions used in competition are custom-written and arranged. The competition selection is required to show a wide variety of skills and emotions. Often, the custom composition is also chosen to highlight the ensemble's strengths and mask its weaknesses.

Like the musical book or composition, the visual presentation of the indoor percussion ensemble is custom-written for each group. Competing indoor percussion ensembles tend to develop their own musical and visual personality and will perform music and visual routines that reflect that style. Some indoor percussion ensembles select a musical/visual book that reflects a specific theme. For example, in 2005, the always entertaining Father Ryan High School of Nashville, Tennessee, selected a musical book with a basketball theme. During the performance, the indoor percussion ensemble performed the music while doing movement routines that created an exciting basketball atmosphere. Their "basketball" show even included a chair being thrown, a clear reference to the antics of Bobby Knight, a famous college basketball coach.

What Will I Experience? What Can I Expect?

Exhilaration is a word that is often used to describe participation in the indoor percussion season. Like other musicians, the members of indoor

Competitive indoor percussion ensembles draw ideas, influence, and inspiration from many resources. Above, the 2005 Father Ryan High School show used elements from the sport of basketball to create a highly entertaining show.

percussion ensembles get a charge out of playing together, especially in front of an audience. One of the differences between marching bands and indoor percussion ensembles is the close proximity of the audience. Because indoor percussion competitions usually take place in a gym, and sometimes a small one, it is likely that the ensemble will perform just a few feet from the front row of the audience.

Drumming gets in one's blood. It is no different for the fans who attend indoor percussion contests. They share this love for drumming and are quick to show their appreciation for it.

As a percussionist, there are few feelings that rival the exhilaration you get when performing with your peers, giving a complete effort, applying all you have learned, putting on an outstanding performance, and exiting the gym floor feeling great about your performance. This feeling is magnified when your excellent performance is recognized by your instructors, the audience, and the judges. Your instructors will quickly praise your efforts after the performance, the audience will salute your outstanding performance with loud applause and cheers, and the judges will reward your efforts with a high score and positive comments.

During the indoor season, you prepare each week for the weekend competition. Judges' feedback from the last contest helps you prepare for the upcoming competition. The judges' feedback will come to you in the form of judging sheets, recorded comments made during your performance, the score you receive, and a critique—typically in a meeting the judges will have with your instructor—after the competition.

Competitive indoor percussion ensembles compete on weekends during the winter months. With each weekend performance, members of indoor percussion ensembles improve their skills and level of achievement.

You will find your skills and confidence getting stronger as you give a 100-percent effort at each rehearsal and performance. With each rehearsal you climb to a new level of playing. Each week, your director will lay out goals and you will work hard to achieve them. You can think of each weekend competition as a test of your knowledge and mastery of skills. For many, this way of learning and achieving goals can easily be applied to regular school work. Many members of both indoor percussion ensembles and winter guards are on their school honor roll.

CHAPTER
2

Drum Corps

Much older than the recent indoor percussion ensemble movement, the modern drum corps (short for drum and bugle corps) has existed since the early 1970s. However, drum corps have been around for centuries in one form or another.

Drum corps have their roots in the military. During the nineteenth century, drums, fifes, and bugles were used to

From their military roots, modern drum corps have evolved into highly skilled and entertaining units. Though they barely resemble their predecessors, drum corps carry on with the same level of dedication and spirit.

signal troops. Specifically, drums were used to control the tempo of troop movement and to intimidate enemies, bugles were used to signal soldiers, and fifes were helpful for parading troops from one location to another. Flags were also used as a method of communication to direct troop movement. As warfare became more sophisticated and new ways of communication were developed, drums, fifes, bugles, and flags became limited to ceremonial and parade duties.

Following World War I and World War II, soldiers returning from duty joined veterans posts, which are social groups for veterans of foreign wars. In order to continue in camaraderie with fellow soldiers, many veterans who learned to play the bugle or drum during wartime formed drum and

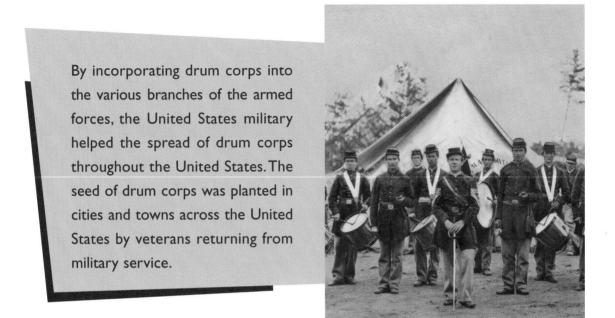

By incorporating drum corps into the various branches of the armed forces, the United States military helped the spread of drum corps throughout the United States. The seed of drum corps was planted in cities and towns across the United States by veterans returning from military service.

bugle corps within their posts. These drum and bugle corps participated in patriotic celebrations, ceremonies, parades, and concerts. Eventually, they began to organize competitions among the various corps. At the same time veterans were forming drum corps for adults, many churches, communities, and youth organizations began sponsoring drum and bugle corps for local youths. It is estimated that by the 1950s, several thousand drum and bugle corps existed in the United States and Canada.

The Modern Drum Corps

Though several variations of drum corps exist, this discussion focuses on those groups that are part of the Drum Corps International (DCI).

Modern drum and bugle corps use instruments that are similar to those used by high school and college marching bands. The marching euphonium is used by both drum corps and marching bands.

DCI governs most of the standards and competitions for high school drum corps. According to DCI, the modern drum corp is an independent youth organization that is "made up of up to 135 14- to 22-year-olds who spend the summer rehearsing and performing an 11-minute show in which they play a variety of horns and percussion instruments, or spin flags, rifles, sabers, and other instruments, all while marching around a football field."

The modern drum and bugle corps is limited to brass and percussion instruments. Earlier brass instruments were bugles that had no valves or only one valve. Today, the bugles used by drum corps actually resemble many of the instruments used in marching bands. Drum corps and marching bands also use similar percussion instrumentation and compete on football-size fields. The primary difference between the two pageantry arts is that, unlike the marching bands, the drum corps do not include woodwind instruments. The brass for a drum and bugle corps consist of trumpets, mellophones, baritones, euphoniums, and tubas. The percussion instruments for a drum and bugle corps are basically the same ones that are used in indoor percussion ensembles.

Drum corps are always evolving. Drum corps are now amplifying their concert percussion instruments and experimenting with electronics. Also present in the drum and bugle corps are color guard units. These units use flags, rifles, and sabers, as well as dance to visually enhance the drum and bugle show.

The Drum Corps Schedule

Drum corps rehearse throughout the winter and compete during the summer months of June, July, and August. The season ends in time for members to return to school.

Drum and bugle corps compete with one another across the nation. Typically, drum corps travel (tour) in the summer throughout the United States and Canada. Some have traveled overseas to Japan and Europe (drum corps exist in many parts of the world, including Asia, Africa, and Europe). The culmination of the drum corps season is the DCI finals in August, when the best drum and bugle corps in the world compete for the international title.

Drum and bugle corps tour the United States and Canada to compete with each other throughout the months of June, July, and August. For fans of drum corps, it is a yearly ritual to follow these exciting groups as they make their way to their ultimate destination, the DCI World Championships.

Drum and bugle corps perform on football fields. The DCI finals are usually held in a large college football stadium or professional football stadium. Each year, the competition gets tougher and tougher as drum corps improve their skills. Percussion companies that produce marching percussion, concert percussion, drum heads, drum sticks, and percussion keyboard mallets are very involved in the competitions. They create improved instruments, sponsor a number of drum corps, sponsor Drum

Corps International, and use a number of drum corps and instructors to test new equipment.

The Drum Corp Experience

Like the members of indoor percussion ensembles, drum corps participants work very hard to improve their skills, learn the music, perfect drill formations, and perform at a high level. The obvious difference between indoor percussion ensembles and drum corps (also known as outdoor percussion) is that drum corps rehearse and perform outside (unless poor weather conditions prevent this from happening). Also, drum and bugle corps compete in the summer, and indoor percussion ensembles compete in the winter.

The performance space (or stage) of the drum corps and the indoor percussion ensemble are very different. A drum and bugle corps performance covers the space of a football field. This requires a great amount of physical exertion, especially during rehearsals when a drill move or entire song is rehearsed over and over for several hours. The drum and bugle corps may rehearse a drill move that will take the musician to a new spot (coordinate) several yards away in just a few seconds. The drummers will then have to pause, listen to instruction from the instructors (both visual and musical instructors), "run it back," and then execute the drill move again. This is often repeated several times until a particular drill move is perfected.

The intensity of a drum and bugle corps season is quite a contrast from that of the indoor percussion ensemble. The time requirements

The Blue Devils, one of America's leading drum corps, perform at the 2002 DCI World Championships in Madison, Wisconsin. Many drum and bugle corps perform night after night in various cities across the United States and Canada during the competitive season.

for a drum and bugle corps may be light in the winter (one weekend a month), but they become extremely intense in the summer. When the drum and bugle corps begins its competitive tour, it will compete every night, be bused to a new state overnight, grab a quick nap and meal, then rise for a long day of rehearsing. This hectic pace continues over the course of several weeks with an occasional break.

It is quite a demanding routine, but the instruction, audiences, adjudication, and performances make it worthwhile. Percussionists who participate in drum and bugle corps receive excellent instruction from nationally recognized teachers. Many of these instructors have marched in drum and bugle corps themselves, attended university schools of music, and spent many years practicing, instructing, and writing, as well as perfecting their teaching skills.

The audiences for drum and bugle corps are very committed to the art. They enthusiastically attend drum corps shows, many times following their favorite corps from city to city during a tour. They tailgate before competitions, wear their favorite corps T-shirt, watch rehearsals between competitions, and trade their favorite drum and bugle corps stories. Many of the fans of drum and bugle corps are very familiar with the history of the activity. They read periodicals such as *Drum Corps World* and search the Internet for the many Web sites now dedicated to drum and bugle corps.

The officials, or judges, of drum and bugle corps competitions are known as adjudicators. These adjudicators are some of the best evaluators in the world of pageantry. Many are former drum corps members and instructors. They attend workshops and clinics in order to be accurate and consistent in their evaluation.

The performance experience for members of drum and bugle corps is incredible. Besides the great audience, the participants enjoy the atmosphere of the large and famous college or professional football stadiums in which many of the championships are held. Many wonderful

Once bitten by the drum corps bug, young men and women from all over the world will spend endless hours in preparation for the Drum Corps International World Championships. All their work will pay off in an outstanding performance that will leave both the performer and spectator breathless.

memories are made at these competitions. The musicians, at the height of their abilities and prepared for the competition, often perform beyond even what they believed was possible. All the work, the sweat, the long hours, and the endless repetition are rewarded by an exhilarating performance that leaves the performer breathless but energized.

For the members of drum and bugle corps, the day of a competition is filled with routines that lead up to the magical moment when they give every ounce of energy in an all-out performance. The rehearsals, preparing their instruments, transporting the equipment to the stadium, the preperformance warm-up in the stadium parking lot (sometimes in front of several hundred people), the march under the grandstands, and entering the stadium at field level all get etched into performers' memories, where they will stay for the rest of their lives. For many drum corps participants, there is no comparison to the exhilaration of entering the field at the international championship, with thousands of fans in the grandstands, performing a near flawless show, and leaving the field knowing they have done their best.

CHAPTER 3

Getting Involved

Perhaps you're interested in joining an indoor percussion ensemble or drum corps but don't know where to begin. There are many ways of getting the information you will need. For example, if you have seen a group perform live, such as at a concert, parade, football halftime show, or competition, you can start by asking the members or director how to get involved.

Drum corps members and your school music instructor may be your best resource for finding information regarding drum and bugle corps and indoor percussion ensembles.

However, your own school music instructor may be your best resource. If a percussion program is available at your school, you may be allowed to participate if you meet the program's requirements. If your school does not have a percussion program, the music instructor may be able to point you in the right direction to find the information you need. Of course, a search on the Internet will reveal many related Web sites. Your school media center specialist may be very helpful in your Internet search.

Most competitive indoor percussion programs start in high school. Usually, students trying out (or auditioning) for these programs probably have already studied music in elementary or middle school and are part of the school's band program. However, this is not always the case. Some directors will allow a student with no previous experience, knowledge, or skills to join an ensemble if the student demonstrates a great attitude and a willingness to learn. Members of indoor percussion ensembles and drum corps have to demonstrate that they are willing to accept criticism and learn, are willing to follow directions, can work with a team, and will remain positive, even if the going gets tough.

Joining an Ensemble or Corps

If you are interested in joining a drum corps or independent indoor percussion ensemble, it will take a little more effort to obtain audition information unless the director of the group happens to teach at your school. However, Drum Corps International's Web site (http://www.dci.org) is a good resource for information about joining a drum and bugle corps.

Most indoor percussion ensembles and drum corps host a preseason information meeting, post information online, or prepare an information packet that you can pick up or have mailed to you. The information usually includes the expectations of the group, required documents, a rehearsal and performance schedule, cost and expenses (membership fee), fundraising information, and background information about the group.

Before you attend auditions for the ensemble or corps, look over the rehearsal schedule and make sure that you can commit to it. If you have a possible conflict with the schedule, be up-front with the director. Some conflicts may be resolved if they are addressed in advance. Obviously, emergencies such as accidents or illness occur. Always contact the director as soon as possible if you are unable to meet the schedule obligations because of an emergency.

Many ensembles have a membership fee, which covers the cost of operating the ensembles. Because many competitive percussion groups travel to different cities, there are costs involved in transporting the members, instructors, and equipment. There are also costs to pay staff members, pay for the show, maintain and purchase equipment, and cover contest entry fees. These costs are covered in part or whole by the membership of the ensemble, depending on whether the ensemble is connected to a school corporation—drum corps usually are not—and the portion of the cost the school can cover. The balance of the cost that is not covered by the membership fee is covered by sponsorships. Each member is required to raise his or her "fair share" in the group's fundraisers. If you have difficulty meeting the financial obligations, be honest with the director and be specific about the problem. Also, every ensemble has required forms. These may include parent consent forms and health forms. Be sure to turn in all forms at the audition.

What Playing Skills Are Required?

The information packet that drum corps and indoor percussion ensembles make available to prospective members is likely to include audition information covering required musical exercises and examples. These

You can learn what to prepare for a music audition by contacting the director of the prospective ensemble for information and an audition packet.

exercises and examples will give you a good idea about the musical expectations of the group. Practice these exercises until you have them memorized.

If you cannot play all the exercises, do not panic. Most audition packets include exercises that are at several different levels so the instructors can correctly assess and place members of the ensemble. Like a sport team that has many players in different positions, indoor percussion ensembles and drum corps have many different positions that need to be filled. Do your best to prepare for the audition by looking over the material in advance and spending the time needed to be thoroughly prepared.

Playing percussion involves being able to execute a basic set of skills known as rudiments. If this is new to you, you may want to seek out a

You should consider working with a qualified instructor to assist you in preparing your audition music. Your school band director or guidance counselor can assist you in finding a qualified instructor from your community.

qualified individual to instruct you one on one. A great idea is to ask the director or a staff member of the group you are auditioning for to work with you in preparing for the audition. It is important to listen to and take direction from the instructor. He or she may have to decide if it is better to work on basic skills before audition material is covered.

If you are entering the ensemble as a beginner, there will be a place for you. Indoor percussion ensembles and drum corps have many positions. If you are new to music but exhibit a great attitude, the director may be able to find a position for you. As you participate in the ensemble you can learn and improve your skills. You will be able to move up to new levels of responsibility once your skills improve.

For any pageantry activity, it is a good idea to be as physically fit as possible before the start of the season. You will be exerting a lot of energy at rehearsals. Marching percussion involves carrying drums, which will put pressure on your back, abdominal muscles, shoulders, hips, and legs. Any exercises you can do to strengthen these muscles is a good idea. Before you begin any new physical activity or sport, it is a good idea to see your family doctor for a physical. You don't want poor physical conditioning to interfere with your ability to be a contributing member of the ensemble.

Preparing for the Audition

Practice daily when preparing for the audition. This daily practice routine is needed to acquire the skills and to strengthen the muscles needed for playing. The more you practice, the more likely you are to improve.

Practicing correctly is essential. Having the director or staff member design a practice routine for you is critical. Your practice routine should include working on basic rudiments, which for a drummer includes rolls, flams, drags, and combinations of these rudiments. You should start the rudiment slowly, then increase the speed, before eventually slowing down again. This practice method is called a rundown.

You should practice all audition material with a metronome. This will help you maintain a steady tempo. If you are auditioning for a marching

Drumming Rudiments

Rudiments can be thought of in two ways. First, they are the fundamentals of drumming and striking the drum. As such, rudiments consist of various sticking combinations that drummers need to know to play drums. A second way to think of rudiments is as the drummers' language. A correctly executed rudiment has a distinctive sound, almost like a word in a language. As you combine these words (rudiments), you create musical sentences (called phrases). By combining several rudiments, solos are created.

The roll is executed by striking a drum and letting the sticks bounce to hit the drum again, causing two quick strokes. When this is done successively with the right and the left sticks, the result is a fast, closed sound coming from the drum line. A flam is executed by striking the drum with both sticks almost at the same time. The first stick strikes the drum from a low height and the second stick immediately strikes the drum after the first stick, but from a high height. The result is an accented, thick drum sound. A ruff is similar to a flam, but the first stick to strike the drum is executed earlier and allowed to bounce. This causes a rhythmic effect. The roll, flam, and ruff are only three of the basic drumming rudiments. By practicing rudiments, you will strengthen your hands and gain better control of your drumming.

percussion position such as marching snare drum, tenor drums (trios, quads, or quints), bass drum, or field cymbals, you should mark time as you play the exercises. You should also devote a little time in your practice routine to sight-reading. Sight-reading is playing an exercise for the first time, not having seen it before. If you are a new musician, spend time with the fundamentals of music, including counting.

The Audition

It is important to show up for the audition as prepared as possible. Do not worry if there are parts of the audition music you cannot play. Just do your best. Also, you should have an open mind when you try out for the ensemble. You may think you would like to play a certain instrument. However, if you're assigned another instrument, give it a chance. You may enjoy it.

Remember, the percussion ensemble is a team. Not everyone has the same responsibility, but every part is important. If a part or position wasn't important, it wouldn't be included in the ensemble. The great opportunity of the percussion ensemble is there are many parts with many different levels or types of responsibilities. You may not qualify for a

Rudimental knowledge is essential to speaking the language of drumming. Percussionists combine rudiments to create musical phrases and sentences that speak to the audience.

Variety is the spice of life. Percussionists are fortunate in that they get to perform on a variety of instruments to create a complete musical picture.

difficult part such as snare drum, but you can become a member of the ensemble on a less demanding instrument. As time progresses, you can continue to improve your skills and audition the next season for a particular part. The makeup of the ensemble allows many players at different levels to participate. In the percussion ensemble, there is a spot for everybody.

Show up with the necessary equipment for the audition. While the ensemble may provide an instrument for the audition, you may have to provide your own sticks or mallets. Also, be sure to show up on time for the audition and have all the necessary paperwork. Be polite during the audition process.

Remember, the director is trying to fill out the entire ensemble. You may have a piano background and thus be asked to play a percussion keyboard or you may have a skill in tuning instruments and be selected to play the timpani. You should always keep in mind that the percussion ensemble is a team that works together to achieve the same goal.

The Rehearsals

Once you make the team, the hard work and the fun begin. You'll spend a lot of time in rehearsal before your first performance. Rehearsals are crucial, and it is important for you to follow through on your commitment to the corps. Rehearsals are usually mandatory, and you should never miss a rehearsal unless you are ill or an emergency occurs.

Show up to rehearsals with enough time to get yourself and your instrument prepared. You should expect rehearsals to begin and end on time. Stretch before practice and be sure to take water to rehearsals. Wear the correct clothing. If you are a member of a drum corp or play a marching percussion instrument in an indoor percussion ensemble, you will need to dress comfortably. Be sure to wear a supportive and comfortable pair of shoes and socks. Indoor percussion ensembles may have specific requirements regarding footwear since many of them practice on a tarp. (They practice on a tarp to prevent damage to the floor of the school's gymnasium.)

Show up to rehearsals prepared. You should have all musical exercises learned up to the correct tempo. You should have any performance music or show music memorized. If you are new to the ensemble and are a beginner, there are drumming exercises and warm-ups to elevate your skills. Also, through auditions, you will be placed on an instrument you

The indoor percussion ensemble employs a wide variety of instruments and thus a wide variety of techniques and skill levels. Whatever your skill level, you can find a role in the indoor percussion ensemble.

are capable of handling. This is one of the positive elements of percussion ensemble; there are a variety of parts for every talent level. You will find that many of the rehearsals early in the season are devoted to developing playing and movement skills.

A positive attitude is important for rehearsals. You have to be ready to accept criticism and give your best at each rehearsal. You want to work hard and have the instructors push you to be your best. Only then will you realize your full potential and perform with excellence. Show up to practice with a clear mind. If you have any problems outside of the ensemble, leave them at the door. Clear your mind of all personal problems so you can fully concentrate during the rehearsal. Also, get plenty of rest between rehearsals. Take care of your life outside of the ensemble so you can give your full effort at each rehearsal.

The Performance

The performance is the payoff for being a part of an ensemble, whether it is an indoor percussion ensemble or drum corps. The day of a performance is a magical day. You will have many special moments. No matter how much you plan and practice, some unexpected moments are likely to occur. Sometimes the best memories come from the unexpected and your ensemble's ability to handle the situation. Enjoy these times with your friends—they are priceless.

Prepare as much as you can the night before. If you have to have any special clothing, a sack lunch, spending money, etc., prepare it the night before and not when it is time to leave home for the practice site. Arriving a little early is always a good idea. Be helpful when you arrive. Ask the director what you can do to help prepare the group.

Most groups will arrive at the practice site early, have a good rehearsal, load their equipment trucks, eat a meal, board a bus, and head toward the performance site. If it is far away, you will probably arrive early enough to stretch, change into your uniform, warm up, and perform. Some trips will be overnight. Your director will provide you with an itinerary

The presentation of music in motion makes indoor percussion and drum corps a truly unique art form.

in advance that will give a complete schedule, directions to the performance site, and any important information.

There are many performance opportunities, and they are all equally important. Besides competitions, ensembles can perform at parades, concerts, and school events, among others.

The indoor percussion ensemble competition and drum corps competition will involve several groups performing (some in different divisions), with the results being announced at the end. This can be a nerve-racking experience. You may perform early in the competition and have to wait several hours to find out the results.

Hopefully, the competition will be very organized and run smoothly. This is not always the case. Keep a positive attitude at the contest site and demonstrate the best manners. Be gracious to the contest host and workers, as well as your fellow competitors. Be a champion on and off of the competition floor or field.

If you have a chance to watch other groups, politely applaud their performances. Remember, you will be on the floor and want people to applaud for you. If you pass other groups in transit to the performance area, wish them good luck. A spirit of cooperation and camaraderie should be present at the competition. If you make comments regarding another groups' performance, keep them positive. Find the good in everything.

The competition is a stressful time for many, and people handle stress in different ways. Some don't handle it very well. If you come across a person who is not handling the stress well, give him or her room. If you have to deal with him or her, smile and be calm. Hopefully your calmness will help the person get a handle on the situation.

There is nothing better than the performance. The feeling you get, the exhilaration, and the memories will last longer than the scores. However, if it is a competition, scores and/or placing will be announced at the end of the contest. Remember, judging a contest is not an exact science. It is subjective—in other words, the judge's opinion. Though it seems to be getting better all the time, judging and the results the judges come up with can be frustrating and confusing. Don't let the results keep you from giving your best and enjoying the moment. Long after you have forgotten the scores, you will remember the feeling you had while performing.

Following the performance is the long bus ride home. This is time to relax, hang out with your friends, talk about the show, or take a nap.

CHAPTER 4

The Benefits of Indoor Percussion and Drum Corps

Participation in indoor percussion ensembles and drum corps has been very rewarding for many students. As mentioned before, it is often said that drumming gets into one's blood. Besides the exhilaration and the satisfaction that you can gain from being a part of a percussive unit, the lessons that you learn and the habits that you form in rehearsals and performance can also make you a better person. For

Members of competitive percussion groups are trained to perform with excellence and, quite often, a certain flair. Each successful performance instills confidence in the unit as a whole and in the individual members.

example, membership in percussion ensembles and drum corps reinforces values such as team work, commitment, dedication, and perseverance. Also, for members who are interested in music careers, these activities provide a realistic example of the life of a traveling musician.

If you're in an indoor percussion ensemble, you are probably representing your school. Your parents, the school, and the community will take pride in your hard work and dedication. If you are part of a drum corps, you are going to meet drummers from many areas of your region. Some drum corps even have members from countries outside of the United

2005 WORLD CHAMPIONS

wgi
SPORT OF THE ARTS

PERCUSSION INDEPENDENT WORLD CLASS

The qualities necessary to create a successful ensemble performance teach the participating musicians many valuable life lessons. All participants of the indoor percussion ensembles and drum corps conclude a season of competition as winners with the valuable skills they have learned.

States. You may also get the chance to travel across the United States and sometimes to other countries.

Students involved in indoor percussion ensembles and drum corps tend to have very successful lives outside of the ensemble. They learn to organize their time, which allows them to maintain a high grade-point average during the busiest part of the season. Many maintain part-time jobs and stay involved with their families. Participating in this activity improves students' social skills as their self-esteem grows. Many participants of indoor percussion ensembles and drum and bugle corps are leaders of their school band.

The Percussion Ensemble as a Career

You may enjoy the indoor percussion ensemble or drum corps so much you would like to pursue it as a career. There are a few professional ensembles in the United States, one of which is Hip Pickles, which performs at professional sporting events and percussion clinics. Groups such as Hip Pickles are few and far between. Most members of indoor percussion ensembles or drum corps pursue the activity as a career by becoming instructors and writers for different groups. Many supplement their income by teaching private lessons and writing for other groups. Some former ensemble members take the skills they have developed and apply them to other musical outlets such as playing in bands, solo and recording careers, instrument design, or retail.

As interest and participation in indoor percussion ensembles and drum corps grow, more individuals will be needed to run competition circuits that host events such as local and national competitions. Other individuals familiar with the activity have established careers helping groups with travel arrangements. Some have provided services assisting groups to raise the funds they need to compete. A few lucky individuals are actually in full-time positions running ensembles and taking care of logistic and business needs.

The opportunity to perform in a unique pageantry activity with dedicated team members, instructors, supporters, and fans makes the world of indoor percussion ensemble and drum corps a truly rewarding experience.

Judges and adjudicators will always be needed. People with the ability to accurately evaluate performances will be held in high demand. As the activity grows, the demand for judges will increase.

Thanks to indoor percussion ensembles and drum corps, an entire new market has opened for drum manufacturers, as well as companies that produce sticks, mallets, and drum heads. These companies are looking for individuals to promote their products through instructional clinics. The companies are also looking for individuals with indoor percussion ensemble and drum corps experience to help design, test, and market products for this new pageantry art.

The indoor percussion ensemble and drum corps are exhilarating and rewarding opportunities waiting for you. If you are one of the fortunate ones who become involved, the memories you will gain will be your greatest reward. Through these activities, you can build strong, long-lasting friendships. The nonmusical qualities you will learn, such as teamwork and goal-setting, will carry you far in life.

Glossary

baritone A large bell front brass instrument that is smaller than the euphonium. The baritone produces a tone that is within the tenor range.

color guard A section of a marching band or drum and bugle corps that performs routines using flags, rifles, sabers, and dance.

concert class A classification within Winter Guard International denoting groups that do not include movement in their show. Groups will use standard concert instruments and not use marching percussion instrumentation.

concert percussion Percussion instruments used in a standard orchestra including percussion keyboards, large bass drum, cymbals, tambourines, and triangles.

drags A drum rudiment that is executed by striking the drum from a low height and allowing the stick to bounce, followed by an accented strike from the opposite stick from a higher height. This is executed in one motion with the first strike occurring early enough to create a rhythmic effect.

euphonium A large bell front brass instrument that is smaller than the tuba. The euphonium produces a tone that is between the tenor and bass range. This instrument is used in drum and bugle corps.

exhilaration Excitement, elation, happiness, joy, or delight.

flams A drum rudiment that is executed by striking the drum from a low height, followed by an accented strike from the opposite stick from a higher height. This is executed in one motion, causing a thick accented sound.

independent A classification within the Winter Guard International pageantry organization for units not affiliated with a high school or junior high school.

indoor percussion A general term used for percussion groups that compete indoors during the winter months.

marching percussion A percussion instrument designed for outdoor use. These are utilized in parades and competitions. The instruments are designed to project sound over large areas

mark-time Keeping time by marching in place.

mellophone A mid-sized bell front brass instrument that is larger than the trumpet. The mellophone produces a tone that is similar to a French horn and is in the alto range.

metronome A time-keeping device with various settings and speeds. This device is used by musicians as they practice for the purpose of keeping steady time.

open class A division within Winter Guard International reserved for groups that display intermediate skills.

orchestral transcription The rewriting of an existing orchestral work for a different type of ensemble.

percussion Instruments that produce sound by being struck or shaken.

percussion ensemble A small ensemble that only uses percussion instruments.

roll A drum rudiment that is executed by striking the drum and allowing the stick to bounce, followed by the same type of strike from the opposite stick.

rudiments Fundamentals of drumming involving various patterns and combinations of strokes on the drum.

scholastic A classification within the Winter Guard International pageantry organization for units with members from one school.

trumpet A small-sized bell front brass instrument that is the smallest brass instrument. The trumpet produces a tone that is in the soprano range.

tuba The largest brass instrument. It must be carried on one shoulder in order to be performed in a drum corps. The tuba produces a tone that is in the bass range.

winter guard A general term used for color guards that compete indoors during the winter months.

world class A division within Winter Guard International reserved for groups that display advanced skills.

For More Information

Drum Corps International
470 South Irmen Drive
Addison, IL 60101
(630) 628-7888
Web site: http://www.dci.org

Percussive Arts Society
701 NW Ferris Avenue
Lawton, OK 73507–5442
(580) 353-1455
Web site: http://www.pas.org

Winter Guard International
7755 Pargon Road, Suite 104
Dayton, OH 45459
(937) 434-7100
Web site: http://www.wgi.org

Web Sites

Due to the changing nature of Internet links, the Rosen Publishing Group, Inc., has developed an online list of Web sites related to the subject of this book. This site is updated regularly. Please use this link to access the list:

http://www.rosenlinks.com/team/ipedc

For Further Reading

A History of Drum & Bugle Corps. Madison, WI: Drum Corps World, 2002.

A History of Drum & Bugle Corps, Volume II. Madison, WI: Drum Corps World, 2003.

Burns, Roy. *Elementary Drum Method*. Miami, FL: Henry Adler, Inc., 1962.

Chiefari, Janet. *Introducing the Drum and Bugle Corps*. New York, NY: Dodd, Mead, 1982.

Holston, Kim R. *The Marching Band Handbook*. Jefferson, NC: McFarland, 2004.

Maffit, Rocky, Chris Brown, and Evelyn Glennie. *Rhythm & Beauty: The Art of Percussion*. New York: Billboard Books, 2005.

Bibliography

A History of Drum & Bugle Corps, Volume II. Madison, WI: Drum Corps World, 2003.

"About DCI." Drum Corps International. Retrieved September 2005 (http://www.dci.org/about).

Winter Guard International. Various articles. Retrieved September 2005 (http://wgi.org).

Index

A

adjudicators, 19, 33, 57
auditions, 38, 39–41, 42–47

C

commitment, 4, 7, 38, 47
competition
  feedback from, 23
  history of, 17–19
  music for, 21
  rules/judging, 18–19, 20, 33, 51
  seasons, 4, 8, 29, 31

D

drum corps
  about, 25, 28–29, 31–32
  benefits of, 33, 35, 52–55, 57
  as a career, 55–57
  competitions, 29–30, 31, 32–35, 50–51
  history of, 25–27, 33
  how to get involved, 36–42
Drum Corps International, 27–28, 29,
    30–31, 38

I

indoor concert percussion ensembles, 14, 20
indoor movement percussion ensembles,
    14, 20
indoor percussion ensembles
  benefits of, 21–24, 52–55, 57
  as a career, 55–57
  competitions, 8, 14, 17, 50–51
  how to get involved, 36–42

M

musical book, 20–21
musical instrument families, 9–10

N

noncompetitive performances,
    15–16, 21

P

pageantry arts, 6
percussion instruments
  defined, 9
  types of, 10–11
performances, 49–51

R

rehearsals, 31, 35, 47–49
required skills, 39–42
rudiments, 40, 42, 43

S

sight-reading, 45
steel drums, 12–13

V

visual presentation, 21

W

winter guard, 15, 19–20, 24
Winter Guard International, 19, 20

About the Author

Daniel Fyffe is the director of bands for Franklin Central High School in Indianapolis, Indiana, and a member of the Winter Guard International Percussion Advisory Board. He is a founding member and former president of the Indiana Percussion Association, as well as a member of the Percussive Arts Society, the Indiana Music Educators Association, and the Indiana State Teachers Association. He also serves on the Indiana Music Educators Association Honor Band Committee and is on the Indiana State School Music Association Percussion Solo & Ensemble Committee. He has accumulated several state and world titles working with various programs, including the prestigious Franklin Central Percussion Symphony. He is endorsed by Promark Sticks and Mallets, Evans Drum Heads, Dynasty Drums, and Sabian Cymbals.

Series Consultant: Susan Epstein

Photo Credits

Cover, pp. 5, 7, 25, 30, 32, 34, 48 Ron Walloch; title page, pp. 16, 24, 44, 46, 50, 56 Winter Guard International; pp. 8, 9, 15, 22, 28, 54 Bateman Photography; pp. 11, 26 Dynasty USA/DEG; p. 13 © David Grossman/Photo Researchers, Inc.; p. 17 Sharon Dunten Photography; p. 18 Tower Studio; p. 27 © Bettmann/Corbis; p. 36 Icon Sports Media; p. 37 Jose Fernandez; p. 40 © Tony Freeman/Photo Edit; p. 41 Dan Fyffe; pp. 52, 53 Hans Kloppert.

Designer: Gene Mollica; Editor: Wayne Anderson; Photo Researcher: Marty Levick